The Parish Companion Prayer Book

Prayers, Meditations and Litanies

Compiled by Fr. Cávana. G. Wallace

As used at St. Margaret Parish, Oceanside, California

The Parish Companion Prayer Book
From various sources in the public domain.
Artwork: James Tissot (1836 –1902)

Mediations on the Holy Mass
Copyright © 2013 by Cávana G. Wallace

ISBN 978-1-300-85430-2

Table of Contents

PRAYERS FOR EVERY DAY

The Lord's Prayer

Our Father, who art in heaven,
hallowed be thy name;
thy kingdom come;
thy will be done on earth
as it is in heaven;
give us this day
our daily bread;
and forgive us our trespasses,
as we forgive those who
trespass against us;
and lead us
not into temptation;
but deliver us from evil.
Amen.

The Hail Mary

Hail Mary, full of grace;
the Lord is with thee;
blessed art thou
among women,
and blessed is the fruit of thy
womb, Jesus.
Holy Mary, Mother of God,
pray for us sinners,
now, and at the hour
of our death. Amen.

The Glory Be

Glory be to the Father,
and to the Son,
and to the Holy Spirit,
as it was in the beginning,
is now and ever shall be,
world without end. Amen.

Daily Offering

O Jesus, through
the Immaculate Heart of Mary
I offer You my prayers, works,
joys, and sufferings of this day
in union with the Holy
Sacrifice of the Mass
throughout the world.
I offer them for all the
intentions of Your Sacred
Heart: in thanksgiving for Your
blessings, for the salvation of
souls, in reparation for my sin,
for my family and friends and
in particular for the intentions
of the Holy Father the Pope
and our bishops
throughout the world.

Act of Faith

O my God, I firmly believe
that You are One God in Three
Divine Persons, Father, Son,
and Holy Spirit;
I believe that Your divine Son
became Man and died for our
sins, and that He will come to
judge the living and the dead.
I believe these and all the
truths which the holy Catholic
Church teaches, because You
have revealed them,
who can neither deceive
nor be deceived.

Act of Hope

O my God, relying on
Your infinite goodness and
promises, I hope to obtain
pardon of my sins,
the help of Your grace,
and life everlasting,
through the merits of Jesus
Christ, my Lord and Redeemer.

Act of Charity

O my God, I love You above
all things, with my whole heart
and soul, because You are all-
good and worthy of all love.
I love my neighbor as myself
for the love of You.
I forgive all who have injured
me, and ask pardon of all
whom I have injured.

Act of Contrition
Sorrow for Sin

O my God, I am heartily sorry
for having offended thee, and I
detest all my sins because I
dread the loss of Heaven and
the pains of hell, but most of all
because they offend thee, my
God, who are all-good and
deserving of all my love.
I firmly resolve with the help
of Thy grace, to confess my
sins, to do penance, and to
amend my life. Amen.

Prayer to my Guardian Angel

Angel of God, my guardian
dear / to whom God's love
commits you here / ever this
day be at my side / to light to
guard, to rule to guide.

*Prayer to St. Michael the
Archangel: For all exposed to
danger in the battlefield*

St. Michael the Archangel,
defend us in battle. Be our
protection against the
wickedness and snares of the
devil. May God rebuke him, we
humbly pray: and do thou,
Prince of the heavenly host, by
the power of God, cast down to
hell Satan and all wicked
spirits, who wander the world
seeking the ruin of souls. Amen

PRAYERS FOR SPECIAL OCCASIONS

Prayer of Respect to the Holy Name

O God, who founded the salvation of the human race on the Incarnation
of Your Word, give Your peoples the mercy they implore, so that all
may know there is no other name to be invoked but the Name of Your
Only Begotten Son. Who lives and reigns with You in the unity of the
Holy Spirit, one God, forever and ever. Amen

Prayer to the Holy Spirit

Come, Holy Spirit, fill the hearts of Your faithful
And kindle in them the fire of Your love
L: Send forth Your Spirit, O Lord, and they shall be created
R: And You shall renew the face of the earth

L: Let us Pray:
O God, Who instructed the hearts of the faithful by the light of the Holy
Spirit, Grant us in the same Spirit to be truly wise and ever rejoice in
His consolation. Through Christ, our Lord.   Amen

The Memorare

Remember, O most gracious Virgin Mary,
that never was it known that anyone who fled to thy protection,
implored thy help, or sought thy intercession was left unaided.
Inspired by this confidence, I fly unto thee, O Virgin of virgins, my
mother; to thee do I come, before thee I stand, sinful and sorrowful. O
Mother of the Word Incarnate, despise not my petitions, but in thy
mercy hear and answer me. Amen.

Prayer to St. Joseph

Grant, we pray, almighty God, that by Saint Joseph's intercession Your
Church may constantly watch over the unfolding of the mysteries of
human salvation, whose beginnings You entrusted to his faithful care.
Through our Lord Jesus Christ, Your Son, who lives and reigns with
You in the unity of the Holy Spirit, one God, forever and ever. Amen.

Prayer for Families

O God, who were pleased to give us the shining example of the Holy
Family, graciously grant that we may imitate them in practicing the
virtues of family life and in the bonds of charity, and so, in the joy of
Your house, delight one day in eternal rewards. Through our Lord Jesus
Christ, Your Son, who lives and reigns with You in the unity of the
Holy Spirit, one God, forever and ever. Amen

Prayer for Priests

O Almighty and Eternal Father, look upon the Face of Christ, and for love of Him Who is the eternal High-priest, extend Your love especially on Your priests. Remember, O most compassionate God, that they too share in the weakness of fallen humanity. Continue to stir up in them the grace of their vocation which is in them by the imposition of the Bishop's hands on the day of their ordination to the Holy Priesthood. Keep them close to You, lest the enemy prevail against them, so that they may never do anything in the slightest degree unworthy of their sublime vocation.

O Jesus, I pray You for Your faithful and fervent priests; for Your unfaithful and tepid priests; for Thy priests laboring at home or abroad in distant mission fields; for Thy tempted priests; for Thy lonely and desolate priests; for Thy young priests; for Thy aged priests; for Thy sick priests; for Thy dying priests; for the souls of Thy priests in Purgatory.

But above all I commend to Thee the priests dearest to me: the priest who baptized me; the priests at whose Masses I assisted and who gave me Thy Body and Blood in Holy Communion; the priests who taught and instructed or helped me and encouraged me; all the priests to whom I am indebted in any other way, particularly (*your priest's name here*). O Jesus, keep them all close to Your heart, and bless them abundantly in time and in eternity. Amen. Mary, Queen of the clergy, pray for us; obtain for us many and holy priests. Amen.

Prayer for the Faithful Departed

Lord, have mercy on us.
Christ, have mercy on us.
Lord, have mercy on us.
Holy Souls, *Pray for us.*
For the souls of our families
We pray to You, O God.
For the souls of our friends,
We pray to You, O God.
For the souls of our enemies,
We pray to You, O God.

For the souls of all unbelievers,
We pray to You, O God.
For the souls of all priests,
We pray to You, O God.
For the souls of all the religious,
We pray You, O God.
For the souls of the just,
We pray to You, O God.

For the souls of all sinners,
We pray to You, O God.
For the Holy Souls
in Purgatory,
We pray You, O God.
For souls without
family or friends,
We pray to You, O God.

Almighty and eternal God, we beg You to have mercy on the Holy Souls in Purgatory, especially those for whom we are bound to pray; and we ask You also to listen to the prayers of the Blessed Souls in our behalf. Amen.

Te Deum: The Great Thanksgiving

(A prayer in praise of Sunday and festive occasions)

You are God: we praise you;
You are the Lord: we acclaim you;
You are the eternal Father:
All creation worships you.

To You all angels, all the powers of heaven,
Cherubim and Seraphim,
sing in endless praise:
Holy, holy, holy, Lord, God of
power and might,
heaven and earth are
full of Your glory.

The glorious company
of apostles praise you.
The noble fellowship of prophets praise you.
The white-robed army of martyrs praise you.
Throughout the world the holy Church acclaims you:

Father, of majesty unbounded,
Your true and only Son, worthy of all worship,
and the Holy Spirit, advocate and guide.
You, Christ, are the king of glory,
the eternal Son of the Father.

When You became man
to set us free
You did not spurn
the Virgin's womb.
You overcame the sting of death,
and opened the kingdom of heaven to all believers.
You are seated at
God's right hand in glory.
We believe that You will come,
and be our judge.

Come then, Lord,
and help Your people,
bought with the price of Your own blood,
and bring us with Your saints to glory everlasting.
Save Your people, Lord, and bless
Your inheritance.
Govern and uphold them now and always.
Day by day we bless you.
We praise Your name forever.
Keep us today,
Lord, from all sin.
Have mercy on us,
Lord, have mercy.
Lord, show us Your love and mercy;
for we put our trust in you.
In you, Lord, is our hope:
and we shall never hope in vain.
Amen

Prayer for the Nation

Composed by the first bishop of Baltimore, John Carroll (1735-1815) for George Washington's inauguration as president.

We pray you, O God of might, wisdom, and justice, through whom authority is rightly administered, laws are enacted, and judgment decreed, assist with Your Holy Spirit of counsel and fortitude the President of these United States, that his administration may be conducted in righteousness, and be eminently useful to Your people, over whom he presides; by encouraging due respect for virtue and religion; by a faithful execution of the laws in justice and mercy; and by restraining vice and immorality.

Let the light of Your divine wisdom direct the deliberations of Congress, and shine forth in all the proceedings and laws framed for our rule and government, so that they may tend to the preservation of peace, the promotion of national happiness, the increase of industry, sobriety, and useful knowledge; and may perpetuate to us the blessing of equal liberty.

We pray for the governor of this state, for the members of the assembly, for all judges, magistrates, and other officers who are appointed to guard our political welfare, that they may be enabled, by Your powerful protection, to discharge the duties of their respective stations with honesty and ability.

We recommend likewise, to Your unbounded mercy, all our fellow citizens throughout the United States, that we may be blessed in the knowledge and sanctified in the observance of Your most holy law; that we may be preserved in union, and in that peace which the world cannot give; and after enjoying the blessings of this life, be admitted to those which are eternal. Grant this, we beseech you, O Lord of mercy, through Jesus Christ, our Lord and Savior.

Amen.

PRAYERS AND MEDITATIONS FOR

THE HOLY MASS

Preparation for Mass

You are here, Lord Jesus. You are going to offer Your sacrifice, Your joys, Your sufferings, Your work, Your passion, and Your death. You are here, Lord, with all Your Church and all her offerings. Our Lady is here, presenting the burning love of her young mother's heart. The holy martyrs are here, the martyrs of all the ages, offering their lives; the apostles are here, offering their efforts; and all Christians, offering their joys and sufferings. The children are here, offering You simply their first love. The youthful are here who study and work, offering You their efforts. The engaged couples offering their promises, young husbands and wives, offering their love; the mother presents her hopes to you, the workers their week's labor, the seniors their memories, and the sick and infirm offer You their lives.

And all these offerings of Your family gathered, Lord Jesus, have meaning only because they are joined to Your eternal offering of yourself to Your Father.

Therefore I bring to You my efforts, my sacrifices, my joys and my offerings, my entire life since my last Mass, and bring too, those of the souls with which You allowed me to care for and who are not present.

I am going to receive You Lord into a heart which has not been humble, but which You shall make as tender as Your own; into a heart which has been hardly pure and which You shall purify reflecting Your own; into a heart which is cowardly and which You shall make as brave as yours is; into a heart too often attached to sin, which You shall make clean; into a selfish heart, which You shall open wide for love. Come Lord Jesus.

(From the *Catholic Missal*, 1954)

The Altar, Incense, Candles and Cross

Like Moses, the priest climbs the holy mountain to speak face to face with God. He imitates the Good Shepherd who leads the flock to heaven. He unites himself to Christ the Bridegroom who on Calvary gives His life for His Bride the Church to make her holy.

SEE: The Altar rises up like a mountain.

RELATE: The incense and the flames of the candles remind me of how God manifested Himself to the Old Testament Prophets.

HIS LIFE: Meditate on Jesus taking His disciples up Mount Tabor where a luminous cloud overshadowed them. The Lord's Body is transfigured in the divine light before them.

HIS DEATH: Now consider the Altar as the symbol of Mount Calvary upon which our Savior offers the sacrifice of His Body and Blood on the Cross.

HIS RESURRECTION: Ponder on this as the sacred place where heaven touches earth.

The Sign of the Cross

The priest officiates over the Mass in the Name of God the Father whose priest he is; and in the Name of God the Son, in whose place he is a priest; and in the Name of the Holy Spirit by whom he is a priest.

SEE: The Cross is visibly central. Within the church its shape is repeated in various forms.

RELATE: The movement of my hand recalls that the one God, who is Father, Son and Holy Spirit came from "heaven above" (the forehead) to "earth below" (the chest) to unite Jew (the left shoulder) and Gentile (the right shoulder) by way of the Cross.

HIS LIFE: Remember Christ telling His disciples that they must take up the Cross daily and follow him.

HIS DEATH: Embrace Christ's Cross and ask for strength to carry it.

HIS RESURRECTION: The image of Christ's Body on the Cross before me, hints of Him rising from the dead. I am confident that He is Risen and victorious.

The Lord be with you.
And with your spirit

The priest assures me of God's presence. As he leads the flock he will again and again assure me of this lest I become distracted.

SEE: The priest's hands have been anointed. He lifts them up as he speaks to God.

RELATE: I recall that I am united with fellow Christians and with them I am part of Christ's mystical Body, the Church.

HIS LIFE: Remember how Christ would often gather His disciples around him as a shepherd gathers His flock.

HIS DEATH: Reflect on how Christ extended His arms on the Cross to open up the gates of heaven.

HIS RESURRECTION: I pray for the priest - that the Spirit of Christ's priesthood will always endure in him.

IV

I Confess
Lord have Mercy - Kyrie Elision

Although invited into God's Holy Presence, I know myself to be unworthy.

SEE: I recall and regret sinful acts and personal failures in my obligations as a member of the Christ's mystical Body, the Church.

RELATE: I beat my chest three times recognizing the many times I have hardened my heart and denied Christ.

HIS LIFE: Remember how Christ instructed His disciples to see Him in the least of those around us.

HIS DEATH: Reflect on how Christ, even from His Cross, pleaded with His Father that my sins be forgiven.

HIS RESURRECTION: I ponder on the fact that my salvation in not a private affair. I look for prayerful support and encouragement from the saints whose sacred images surround me, especially our Blessed Mother Mary.

Gloria in Excelsis Deo
Glory to God in the Highest

(Omitted during Advent and Lent)

This is the song of God's Holy Angels.
Their language is sacred.

SEE: The angels surround us and the seraphim look down upon the altar. Guardian angels of everyone are present.

RELATE: God's invisible glory fills the church. It is reflected by gold and silver. The candles and colors remind me of the glory and beauty of heaven.

HIS LIFE: Meditate on the angels appearing to the shepherds and announcing the birth of Christ.

HIS DEATH: Consider how the saints and holy martyrs were courageous in their public witness to Christ.

HIS RESURRECTION: Ponder on what heaven is like - Christ as the King of Glory surrounded by the angels, His Blessed Mother, the holy apostles, and the multitude of saints.

VI

The Lessons from Holy Scripture

SEE: The importance of Holy Scriptures is shown by a special place dedicated for them to be read out loud for all to hear.

RELATE: Attentive listening to the Scriptures allows the Holy Spirit to highlight particular themes or passages that I will remember and take with me.

HIS LIFE: The whole history of the Chosen People as they waited for the Messiah to be reveled is reflected in the Old Testament Scriptures. I also long to see and welcome the Savior.

HIS DEATH: Consider how the Virgin Mary would have known the Psalms by heart, taught them to Jesus in His infancy and how they used them to express their own prayers, hopes and petitions.

HIS RESURRECTION: A New Testament letter from one of the Lord's closest friends is read. These are words to help me find my place in God's family, the Church.

VII

Book of Gospels

SEE: The Altar represents Christ. The Book of the Gospels upon it communicates His Message.

RELATE: The Church sings praise to God praying that she will always be found worthy to proclaim Christ's message to the world.

HIS LIFE: Through the words of His Gospel spoken through His ordained, Christ stands in the presence of His Church. Like incense rising, Christ offers His Gospel message to His heavenly Father for the salvation of the world.

HIS DEATH: By tracing a cross on my forehead, on my lips and over my heart, I commit myself to the same mindset of Christ, not to be afraid to speak in defense of the Faith and take to heart the Gospel message.

HIS RESURRECTION: I listen to the homily based on today's Scriptures or a sermon on an article of faith. I discern how Christ Himself is communicating to me the truth of His Gospel in the circumstances of my life and living.

VIII

I Believe

SEE: I stand to acknowledge this declaration as the concise interpretation of the Holy Scriptures.

RELATE: These articles of faith have been handed down from the earliest days of Christianity. Missionaries have brought the Creed to distant lands; martyrs have given their lives in witness to its truth.

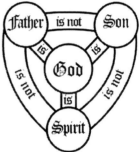

HIS LIFE: I am invited into the knowledge and the life of the mystery of God who is an eternal unity of three - Father, Son and Holy Spirit - the Holy Trinity.

HIS DEATH: I identify myself as a member of Christ's one and unique Church, identified by its union with the historic and true successors of the Apostles, especially with the pope, the successor of St. Peter.

HIS RESURRECTION: I am united with all the saints of heaven, the Church Triumphant, and I long for my own journey's end - to see God face to face in the company of the Blessed Virgin and the hosts of angels.

Preparation of Gifts to Offer

SEE: I offer myself to God - my time, my family life, my work and personal resources to further Christ's mission and ministry through His Church.

RELATE: I place my offerings on the altar with the bread and wine.

HIS LIFE: As incense covers the gifts and covers me, it also rises up to the heavens. This is the direction I also look towards, praying that I will be acceptable in God's sight and able to enter into His presence.

HIS DEATH: I join myself to the sacrifice of Christ, knowing that my heavenly Father will never refuse the offering of His only begotten Son.

HIS RESURRECTION: The priest makes a final prayer over the gifts anticipating that they will, through his words and actions, be changed from tokens of the old order of creation, to the first fruits of the new creation - the Glorious and heavenly Body and Blood of Christ.

Eternal Father, I offer You the sacrifice wherein Your dear Son Jesus offered Himself upon the Cross and which He now renews upon this altar, to adore You and to render to You that honor which is Your due, acknowledging Your supreme dominion over all things and their absolute dependence on You, for You are our first beginning and our last end; to give You thanks for countless benefits received; to appease Your justice provoked to righteous anger by so many sins, and to offer You worthy satisfaction for the same; and finally to implore Your grace and mercy for myself, for all poor sinners, for the whole world, and for the blessed souls in purgatory.

Lift up your Hearts

SEE: As Moses prepared the Chosen People to cross into the Promised Land, the priest directs our attention to the goal of our journey - heaven.

RELATE: We are now pilgrims ready to enter through the gates of the heavenly Jerusalem.

HIS LIFE: It is Christ the Good Shepherd who will now lead us home. Christ is the Gate of the Sheepfold. We must literally go through Him to enter into the very presence of God.

HIS DEATH: We embrace the glorious Cross and long to be able to share in the vision of God, to join the angels of heaven in one prayer of thanks and praise.

HIS RESURRECTION: I ask my guardian angel to guide me closer and closer to the throne of God and to join all the angels of heaven in prayer and praise.

XI

This is my Body – This is my Blood

SEE: The priest has become like Moses. On top of the Holy Mountain, he enters into the cloud of God's presence. The priest, like Christ on the Cross, enters into a dialogue with God the Father on my behalf.

Prayer is made so that I will always remain faithful within Christ's Holy Church whom He identifies as His Bride, having sacrificed Himself on the Cross for her sake.

RELATE: The priest prays like a shepherd as if gathering the faithful from near and far, bringing them into the sacrifice of Christ. To stand in God's presence, I must be purified in mind, body and soul.

Around me are my brothers and sisters. I am joined also to my extended family of the saints in heaven from every walk of life. I unite myself to Mary, Mother of the Church on earth and in heaven.

I see the priest extending his hands over the bread and wine whereby signaling that God takes possession of these offerings which have been set aside for Him. I unite myself with these offerings.

HIS DEATH: The priest stands at the Altar of Sacrifice in the person of Christ the Bridegroom who offers His life to His Bride, the Church. The priest makes his own the words of Christ spoken at the Last Supper over the bread and wine, whereby they are changed in their invisible reality into the very Body and Blood of Christ.

HIS RESURRECTION: In this sacred moment I am being brought into the very center of heaven where Christ reigns over all and continues to offer himself to His Father on my behalf. I am not passive. I offer myself to my heavenly Father praying that He will somehow recognize His Son reflected in me. The saints around God's throne encourage me.

XII

Our Father

SEE: My hands are joined together, over my heart, as if pointing my soul in the direction of heaven. Christ wants me to see His Father. In the Spirit of Christ I acknowledge His Father as my Father also.

RELATE: I join my words, my will and actions to further the Kingdom of God on earth.

HIS DEATH: As Christ died for my sins and has reconciled me to the Father, I commit myself to also forgive in the same measure.

HIS RESURRECTION: Attentive to the voice of the Shepherd, I can avoid all sin and maintain the unity of the family I am a part of. He guides me along the path and points me to the glory and power of heaven.

XIII

The Peace of the Lord

SEE: The priest opens his arms, as if sending forth from the altar the "breath" of Christ's gift of peace.

RELATE: I acknowledge my troubled heart – a heart that has often been wounded by sin and disappointment. I long for a peace only God can give.

HIS DEATH: Christ exposed himself to the violence anger and hatred of the world so that it would not claim us as its prisoner. He has paid the peace offering by His blood.

HIS RESURRECTION: The undeserved gift of true peace of soul I am now offered by Christ. I accept and allow myself to be an agent of God's peace and goodwill to all I meet.

Behold the Lamb of God

SEE: I kneel as the priest raises the Sacred Host. The gates of heaven are opened up before me. I long for the vision of heaven.

RELATE: I cannot trust my eyes, so used to this world they are. I must see with the eyes of faith the invisible and heavenly Christ who stands before me.

HIS DEATH: Christ still bears His wounds on His glorious and resurrected Body.

HIS RESURRECTION: These sacred wounds continue to speak the language of divine love. As I gaze towards God in His holy sanctuary, my own body and soul longs for healing.

Guide for Holy Communion

Holy Communion is reserved for members of the Catholic Church. Although expected to attend Mass every Sunday (unless physically prevented), Catholics are not required to receive Holy Communion every time they attend, although this is the ideal.

When a Catholic does receive, Holy Communion is offered trusting that the member has frequented Confession as necessary (see p.27), is committed to attending weekly Sunday Mass, is able to give a public witness to their Catholic Faith and, if partnered, the relationship is a true Catholic marriage.

Unless dispensed by reason of age or illness, one is also expected to have had fasted from food or drink (with the exception of water), for at least one hour, prior to reception of Holy Communion.

Those not going up to the altar at this Mass may instead find comfort and strength using the words of the following prayer, thereby making a personal and **spiritual communion** instead.

My Jesus, I believe that You are present
in the most Blessed Sacrament.
I love You above all things and
I desire to receive You into my soul.

Since I cannot now
receive You sacramentally,
come at least spiritually into my heart.
I embrace You as if You have already come,
and unite myself wholly to You.
Never permit me to be separated from You.

Amen.

Prayers Before Receiving Holy Communion

From Saint Ambrose of Milan

Lord Jesus Christ, I approach Your banquet table in fear and trembling, for I am a sinner, and dare not rely on my own worth but only on Your goodness and mercy. I am defiled by many sins in body and soul, and by my unguarded thoughts and words.

Gracious God of majesty and awe, I seek Your protection, I look for Your healing. Poor troubled sinner that I am, I appeal to you, the fountain of all mercy. I cannot bear Your judgment, but I trust in Your salvation. Lord, I show my wounds to You and uncover my shame before you. I know my sins are many and great, and they fill me with fear, but I hope in Your mercies, for they cannot be numbered.
Lord Jesus Christ, eternal king, God and man, crucified for mankind, look upon me with mercy and hear my prayer, for I trust in you. Have mercy on me, full of sorrow and sin, for the depth of Your compassion never ends.

Praise to you, saving sacrifice, offered on the wood of the cross for me and for all mankind. Praise to the noble and precious blood, flowing from the wounds of my crucified Lord Jesus Christ and washing away the sins of the whole world.

Remember, Lord, Your servant, whom You have redeemed with Your blood. I repent my sins, and I long to put right what I have done. Merciful Father, take away all my offenses and sins; purify me in body and soul, and make me worthy to taste the holy of holies.

May Your body and blood, which I intend to receive, although I am unworthy, be for me the remission of my sins, the washing away of my guilt, the end of my evil thoughts, and the rebirth of my better instincts. May it incite me to do the works pleasing to You and profitable to my health in body and soul, and be a firm defense against the deceits of my enemies.

From Saint Thomas Aquinas

Almighty and Eternal God, behold I come to the sacrament of Your only-begotten Son, our Lord Jesus Christ. As one sick I come to the Healer of life; unclean, to the Fountain of mercy; blind, to the Light of eternal splendor; poor and needy to the Lord of heaven and earth.

Therefore, I beg of You, through Your infinite mercy and generosity, heal my weakness, wash my uncleanness, give light to my blindness, enrich my poverty, and clothe my nakedness. May I thus receive the Bread of Angels, the King of Kings, the Lord of Lords, with such reverence and humility, contrition and devotion, purity and faith, purpose and intention, as shall aid my soul's salvation.

Grant, I beg of You, that I may receive not only the Sacrament of the Body and Blood of our Lord, but also its full grace and power. Give me the grace, most merciful God, to receive the Body of Your only Son, our Lord Jesus Christ, born of the Virgin Mary, in such a manner that I may deserve to be intimately united with His mystical Body and to be numbered among His members. Most loving Father, grant that I may behold for all eternity face to face Your beloved Son, whom now, on my pilgrimage, I am about to receive under the sacramental veil, who lives and reigns with You, in the unity of the Holy Spirit, God, world without end. Amen.

To the Blessed Virgin

O most blessed Virgin Mary, Mother of tenderness and mercy, I, a miserable and unworthy sinner, fly to you with all the affection of my heart and I seek out your motherly love, that, as you stood by your most dear Son, while He hung on the Cross, so, in your kindness, you may be pleased to stand by me, a poor sinner, and all Priests who today are offering the Sacrifice here and throughout the entire holy Church, so that with your gracious help we may offer a worthy and acceptable oblation in the sight of the most high and undivided Trinity. Amen.

To Saint Joseph

O Blessed Joseph, happy man, to whom it was given the honor, not only to see and to hear the One Whom many kings longed to see and saw not, who longed to hear, and heard not; but also to carry Him in your arms, to embrace Him, to clothe Him, and guard and defend Him. Pray for us, O Blessed Joseph, that we may be made worthy of the promises of Christ.

O God, Who has given us a royal priesthood, we beseech You, that as Blessed Joseph was found worthy to touch with his hands, and to bear in his arms, Your only-begotten Son, born of the Virgin Mary, so may we be made fit, by cleanness of heart and blamelessness of life, to assist at Thy holy altar; may we, this day, with reverent devotion partake of the Sacred Body and Blood of Your Only-begotten Son, and may we in the world to come be accounted worthy of receiving an everlasting reward. Through the same Christ our Lord. Amen.

XVII

Prayers After Receiving Holy Communion

The Anima Christi Prayer

Soul of Christ, sanctify me.
Body of Christ, save me.
Blood of Christ, fill me.
Water from the side of Christ, wash me.
Passion of Christ, strengthen me.
O Good Jesus, hear me.
Within Thy wounds hide me.
Do not let me be separated from You.
From the deadly enemy defend me.
At the hour of my death call me.
And have me come to You,
So that with all Thy saints,
I may praise You forever and ever.
Amen.

From Saint Thomas Aquinas

I give You thanks, Lord, holy Father, almighty and eternal God, who have been pleased to nourish me, a sinner and Your unworthy servant, with the precious Body and Blood of Your Son, our Lord Jesus Christ: this through no merits of mine, but due solely to the graciousness of Your mercy. And I pray that this Holy Communion may not be for me an offense to be punished, but a saving plea for forgiveness.

May it be for me the armor of faith, and the shield of good will. May it cancel my faults, destroy my base instincts and carnal passions, increase charity and patience, humility and obedience and all the virtues, may it be a firm defense against the snares of all my enemies, both visible and invisible, the complete calming of my impulses, both of the flesh and of the spirit, a firm adherence to you, the one true God, and the joyful completion of my life's course.

And I beseech You to lead me, a sinner, to that banquet beyond all telling, where with Your Son and the Holy Spirit You are the true light of Your Saints, fullness of satisfied desire, eternal gladness, consummate delight and perfect happiness. Through Christ our Lord. Amen.

Prayer of Self-Offering

Receive, Lord, my entire freedom. Accept the whole of my memory, my intellect and my will. Whatever I have or possess, it was You who gave it to me; I restore it to You in full, and I surrender it completely to the guidance of Your will. Give me only love of You together with Your grace, and I am rich enough and ask for nothing more. Amen.

The Universal Prayer

Lord, I believe in you:
increase my faith.
I trust in you:
strengthen my trust.
I love you:
let me love You
more and more.
I am sorry for my sins:
deepen my sorrow.

I worship You
as my first beginning,
I long for You as my last end,
I praise You
as my constant helper,
And call on You
as my loving protector.
Guide me by Your wisdom,
Correct me with Your justice,

Comfort me with Your mercy,
Protect me with Your power.

I offer you, Lord, my thoughts:
to be fixed on you;
My words:
to have You for their theme;
My actions:
to reflect my love for you;
My sufferings: to be endured
for Your greater glory.

I want to do what
You ask of me:
In the way You ask,
For as long as You ask,
Because You ask it.

Lord, enlighten my
understanding,
Strengthen my will,
Purify my heart,
and make me holy.

Help me to repent
of my past sins
And to resist temptation
in the future.
Help me to rise above my
human weaknesses
And to grow stronger as a
Christian.

Let me love you,
my Lord and my God,
And see myself as I really am:
A pilgrim in this world,

A Christian called
to respect and love
All whose lives I touch,
Those under my authority,
My friends and my enemies.
Help me to conquer anger

with gentleness,
Greed by generosity,
Apathy by fervor.
Help me to forget myself
And reach out toward others.

Make me prudent in planning,
Courageous in taking risks.
Make me patient in suffering,
unassuming in prosperity.

Keep me, Lord,
attentive at prayer,
Temperate in food and drink,
Diligent in my work,
Firm in my good intentions.

Let my conscience be clear,
My conduct without fault,
My speech blameless,
My life well-ordered.
Put me on guard against my
human weaknesses.
Let me cherish
Your love for me,
Keep Your law,
And come at last
to Your salvation.

Teach me to realize
that this world is passing,
That my true future
is the happiness of heaven,
That life on earth is short,
And the life to come eternal.

Help me to prepare for death
With a proper fear of judgment,
But a greater trust
in Your goodness.
Lead me safely through death
To the endless joy of heaven.

Amen

Prayer to the Blessed Virgin

O Mary, Virgin and Mother most holy, behold, I have received your most dear Son, whom you conceived in your immaculate womb, brought forth, nursed and embraced most tenderly.

Behold Him at whose sight you used to rejoice and be filled with all delight; Him whom, humbly and lovingly, once again I present and offer Him to you to be clasped in your arms, to be loved by your heart, and to be offered up to the Most Holy Trinity as the supreme worship of adoration, for your own honor and glory and for my needs and for those of the whole world.

I ask you therefore, most loving Mother: entreat for me the forgiveness of all my sins and, in abundant measure, the grace of serving Him in the future more faithfully, and at the last, final grace, so that with you I may praise Him for all the ages of ages. Amen. Hail, Mary, full of grace, the Lord is with you; blessed are you among women, and blessed is the fruit of your womb, Jesus. Holy Mary, Mother of God, pray for us sinners now and at the hour of our death. Amen.

Prayer to St. Joseph

Guardian of virgins, and holy father Joseph, to whose faithful custody Christ Jesus, Innocence itself, and Mary, Virgin of virgins, were committed; I pray and beseech you, by these dear pledges, Jesus and Mary, that, being preserved from all uncleanness, I may with spotless mind, pure heart, and chaste body, ever serve Jesus and Mary most chastely all the days of my life. Amen.

HOW TO MAKE A GOOD CONFESSION

This Sacrament allows the repentant sinner

> to formally confess their mortal sins to God.

> to be assured by the priest in the name of God, of the forgiveness of their sins and absolution of any eternal punishments due because of them.

> to receive grace in order to persevere in the Christian life so as to one day reach heavenly perfection.

> By prayers, charity and penance to right any wrongs.

The Duty to Confess Mortal Sins

Although all sin injures the soul and weakens our spiritual defenses, one commits a "mortal" sin by willingly and knowingly violating the Law of God in a serious offense, the consequence of which is the supernatural death of the soul and our withdrawal from friendship with God.

Catholics are duty-bound to repent of and confess to God their mortal sins and receive absolution through the Sacrament of Reconciliation (confession) before receiving Holy Communion.

Preparation Prayer before Confession

Come Holy Spirit into my soul. Enlighten my mind that I may know the sins I ought to confess, and grant me Your grace to confess them fully, humbly and with contrite heart. Help me to firmly resolve not to commit them again. O Blessed Virgin, Mother of my Redeemer, mirror of innocence and sanctity, and refuge of penitent sinners, intercede for me through the Passion of Your Son, that I may obtain the grace to make a good confession.

All you blessed Angels and Saints of God, pray for me, a sinner, that I may repent from my sinful ways, that my heart may henceforth be forever united with yours in eternal love. Amen

EXAMINATION OF CONSCIENCE

The following questions, based on the Ten Commandments, are not a checklist for Confession, but a help to develop a greater capacity for self-knowledge, in order to reflect on your relationship with your soul, with God and your neighbor.

I.   *Giving God His Place*

Do I dedicate my day to God? Do I trust His Love and avoid superstitions? Am I afraid to bless myself in public such as, at meals, in restaurants or when passing a Catholic church? Have I ever received Holy Communion casually or sacrilegiously? Have I ever deliberately told a lie in Confession or withheld confessing a serious sin? Are there other "gods" in my life such as money, security, power, people, preoccupation with my own appearance or reputation, etc.?

II.   *Respect for the Sacred*

Have I used God´s name disrespectfully, carelessly or in anger? Have I been angry with God? Have I wished evil or misfortune upon anyone? Have I insulted, spoken ill of or damaged the reputation of a member of the Catholic clergy. Have I trivialized a blessed and sacred object? Have I partaken in a communion service of a non-Catholic religious group?

III.   *The Lord's Day*

Have I deliberately missed Mass on Sundays or Holy Days? Have I attended a non-Catholic religious service instead of Sunday Mass? Do I prepare my body, my soul and mind for Sunday Mass beforehand? Do I show special respect for Sunday worship by the clothes I wear? Have I tried to arrive on time for Sunday Mass? Am I mindful of not distracting others from prayer during Mass? Do I engage in needless work on Sunday or create unnecessary work for others preventing them from attending Mass or spending time with family?

IV.   *Family Life*

Do I honor and respect my parents and those who have true authority over me? Have I neglected my natural and religious duties to my spouse and children? Have I neglected to see that my children truly know and respect their Catholic faith? Am I embarrassed to pray with my spouse, family or friends or put work before them? Do I attempt to protect my children from immoral dangers to their moral and spiritual life?

V.   *Protecting Human Life*

Have I had an abortion or encouraged, helped, excused or condoned it, even by my silence? Have I wished or physically harmed anyone or sought pleasure in violence. Have I abused alcohol, drugs or food? Have I driven under the influence? Did I provide a bad example to anyone, thereby leading that person into sin? Have I allowed anger to become rage or hatred? Have I willfully altered my body out of vanity? Do I use artificial methods or chemically manipulate my body's natural function in order to avoid future parenthood, such as sterilization, contraception or morning after pills. Have I engaged, in any way, in sins against marriage and human life such as artificial insemination or in vitro fertilization? Have I neglected the medical care of others, or the natural needs of the body in order to hasten death?

VI.   *Loving Relationships*

Have I, as a Catholic, allowed myself to be married by a civil or non-Catholic official? Have I been faithful to my Catholic marriage vows in thought, word and deed? Have I sought for or encouraged civil divorce rather than attempt a true reconciliation? Have I engaged in any sexual activity outside of marriage? Have I used any method of artificial contraception or birth control in my marriage? Have I been guilty of impure acts with myself or with others, or even with my spouse? Do I seek to discipline my thoughts and imagination? Have I supported or condoned unnatural sexual relationships or unions, regardless of their legal or social status? Do I seek to be pure in my thoughts, words and actions? Am I careful in how I dress or communicate myself in public so as not to arouse interest from others?

VII.   *My Belongings*

Have I stolen what is not mine? Have I wasted time at work, school, on social media or on the Internet? Do I gamble with money in such a way that I neglect the needs of others, and take quality time away from family and friends? Do I pay my debts promptly? Do I support the maintenance of the parish church and respond generously to appeals for charity? Have I deceived anyone out of what is justly theirs, for example, with creditors, insurance companies, or just taxes? Have I cheated on tests or in sports, lied on application forms or been dishonest in my studies or business, or infringed upon the legal and natural rights of others.

VIII.   *Integrity*

Have I lied? Do I speak badly of others behind their back? Do I substitute social media for true friendships and relationships? Am I uncharitable in my thoughts and opinions of others? Do I keep secret what should be kept confidential? Have I set out to damage the reputation or credibility of another or engaged in petty revenge to settle scores?

IX.   *Boundaries*

Have I dwelt upon impure thoughts, sights or imaginations? Have I knowingly put myself in an environment that would allow me to be tempted beyond my strength? Have I been careful that my words and actions cannot be construed inappropriately by the vulnerable?

X.   *Being Content*

Am I jealous of what other people have? Do I compete with or envy the families or possessions of others? Am I greedy or selfish? Do I waste money on nonessentials or at the expense of those who deserve my charity? Do I use food or purchases to avoid dealing with issues of my heart or soul? Do I abuse tobacco or alcohol? Have I misused medicine or engaged in illicit drugs or substances. Am I more concerned with my reputation than with eternal life with God?

GOING TO CONFESSION

1.   Plan to arrive at the beginning of the appointed time. Upon entering, begin with *"In the Name of the Father and of the Son and of the Holy Spirit"*. Then say, *"Bless me Father for I have sinned. It has been* (state how long) *since my last confession and these are my sins."*

2.   Confessing one's mortal sins is relatively simple. Simply state the actual sin, recalling how often you might have repeated this offense. Remember, because your preparation involves an examination of your conscience before God, you don't need to go into all the details with the priest. If the priest needs clarification, he knows to ask.

3.   Be careful about using the word "*because*" after confessing a particular sin. It can be easy to blame someone or something else for our own actions. Confess your own sins, not those of others!

4.   Confess actual sins, not your disappointments or anxieties. Remember, sin is *"an utterance, a deed, or a desire contrary to the eternal law."* (Catechism of the Catholic Church, para.1849).

5.   After confessing your sins, the priest might give some words of simple advice. Even though you may have said an act of contrition as part of your examination of conscience, the priest may ask you to say it again, during which he usually begins the words of the Prayer of Absolution - the essential part of which is when he says, *"I absolve you from your sins, in the Name of the Father and of the Son and of the Holy Spirit."*

6.   You respond "*Amen*".

7.   The priest will normally give a penance - usually an act of devotion. Penance is the first thing we do in response to God's mercy. If we are able to repair any damage we have caused by our sins, we should do so. If unable, then one should make up for it in some other way, such as extra time in prayer or by good deeds.

8.   Be grateful that God always forgives the repentant sinner. Pray for those who are going to confession and for the priest through whom God uses to assure us personally of the forgiveness of sins.

PRAYERS AFTER CONFESSION

I thank You, my Heavenly Father, not only for having created me, redeemed me, and called me into safety of Your Holy Church, but still more for having waited for my return when I had wandered far away from you.

I thank You for having often pardoned me, as I hope You have done this day, and for having preserved me from so many other sins, into which I could have fallen had I not been preserved by Your grace.

Although I will not be immune from being tempted by the forces of darkness, I rely on Your strength to defeat all evil. Grant me then, through the merits of Jesus Christ Your Son, the grace and strength of perseverance. The Divine Savior has assured us that whatever we ask in His Name, You will grant it to us. I call upon You, therefore, through all that Your dear Son suffered for me, never to let me forsake You any more. May I have the greatest confidence that, if I continue to pray for this grace, I shall obtain it, because You have promised to hear our prayers.

But I fear that, in some unguarded moment, I should forget my dependence on You, and fail to call out for help, and then relapse into my former ways. Grant me, therefore, that in all my temptations I may have instant resort to You, by calling upon the holy Names of Jesus and Mary. By doing so, my Lord, I may confidently hope to complete my days in Your grace, and to love You forever in heaven, where I shall be sure never to be separated from You, consumed in the light eternal of Your love. Amen

THE ROSARY

The Rosary is made up of twenty "mysteries" (significant events or moments in the life of Jesus and Mary), which are grouped into four "volumes". The first contains *Joyful* mysteries (recited on Mondays and Saturdays); the second, the *Luminous* mysteries of light (Thursdays); the third, the *Sorrowful* mysteries (Tuesdays and Fridays); and the fourth, the *Glorious* mysteries (Wednesdays and Sundays).

HOW TO PRAY THE ROSARY

L: Leader, R: Respond.
If praying alone, fulfill all the parts

L: *In the name of the Father*
and of the Son
and of the Holy Spirit.
R: Amen
L: *O God come to my aid.*
R: O Lord, make haste to help me.
L: *Glory be to the Father, and to the Son and to the Holy Spirit.*
R: As it was in the beginning, is now, and ever shall be, world without end. Amen.
L. *I believe in God the Father Almighty, Creator of heaven and earth; and in Jesus Christ, His only Son, our Lord; Who was conceived by the Holy Ghost, born of the Virgin Mary, suffered under Pontius Pilate, was crucified, died and was buried. He descended into hell. On the third day He arose again; He ascended into heaven and sits at the right hand of God, the Father Almighty; from thence He shall come to judge the living and the dead.*
R: I believe in the Holy Spirit, the Holy Catholic Church, the communion of saints, the forgiveness of sins, the resurrection of the body, and life everlasting. Amen
L: *Our Father, who art in heaven, hallowed be thy name, thy kingdom come, thy will be done on earth as it is in heaven.*
R: Give us this day our daily bread and forgive us our trespasses as we forgive those who trespass against us, and lead us not into temptation but deliver us from evil.   Amen.

L: *We pray Three Hail Mary's for the virtues of*
          Faith, Hope and Charity:
          Hail Mary, Mary, full of grace, the Lord is with thee: blessed
          art thou among women, and blessed is the fruit of thy womb,
          Jesus.

R: Holy Mary, Mother of God, pray for us sinners, now, and at the hour of our death. Amen. *(Repeat two more times)*

L: *Glory be to the Father, and to the Son,*
          and to the Holy Spirit.

R: As it was in the beginning, is now, and ever shall be, world without end. Amen.

L: The *(Joyful/Luminous/Sorrowful/Glorious)* mysteries of Most Holy Rosary of the Blessed Virgin Mary.

       The *(first/second/third/fourth/fifth)* Mystery – the mystery of the *(see Rosary Mysteries below)*

       After a short pause for reflection (examples given below), recite the "Our Father", ten "Hail Marys" and the "Glory be to the Father".

       An invocation may be added after each decade.

————————

THE ROSARY MYSTERIES

Referenced to Scripture and the Catechism of the Catholic Church

∞∞∞∞ **The Joyful Mysteries** ∞∞∞∞

1.   The Annunciation

In the sixth month, the angel Gabriel was sent from God to a city of Galilee named Nazareth, to a virgin betrothed to a man whose name was Joseph, of the house of David; and the virgin's name was Mary" (*Lk* 1:26-27). "The Annunciation to Mary inaugurates the 'fullness of time' (*Gal* 4:4), the time of the fulfillment of God's promises and preparations" (*CCC*, 484).

Our Father, 10 Hail Mary's (contemplating the mystery),
Glory be to the Father.

2.   The Visitation

"In those days Mary arose and went with haste into the hill country, to a city of Judah, and she entered the house of Zechariah and greeted Elizabeth. And when Elizabeth heard the greeting of Mary, the babe leaped in her womb; and Elizabeth was filled with the Holy Spirit and she exclaimed with a loud cry, 'Blessed are you among women, and blessed is the fruit of your womb!'" (*Lk* 1:39-42). "Mary's visitation to Elizabeth thus became a visit from God to His people" (CCC, 717).

Our Father, 10 Hail Mary's (contemplating the mystery),
Glory be to the Father.

3.   The Birth of Our Lord

"In those days a decree went out from Caesar Augustus that all the world should be enrolled. This was the first enrolment, when Quirinius was governor of Syria. And all went to be enrolled, each to his own city. And Joseph also went up from Galilee, from the city of Nazareth, to Judea, to the city of David, which is called Bethlehem, because He was of the house and lineage of David, to be enrolled with Mary, his betrothed, who was with child. And while they were there, the time came for her to be delivered. And she gave birth to her first-born son and wrapped Him in swaddling cloths, and laid Him in a manger, because there was no place for them in the inn" (*Lk* 2:1-7). "Jesus was born in a humble stable, into a poor family. Simple shepherds were the first witnesses to this event. In this poverty heaven's glory was made manifest" (*CCC,* 525).

Our Father, 10 Hail Mary's (contemplating the mystery),
Glory be to the Father.

4.   The Presentation of the Child Jesus at the Temple

"And at the end of eight days, when He was circumcised, He was called Jesus, the name given by the angel before He was conceived in the womb. And when the time came for their purification according to the law of Moses, they brought Him up to Jerusalem to present Him to the Lord (as it is written in the law of the Lord, *'Every male that opens the womb shall be called holy to the Lord'*) and to offer a sacrifice according to what is said in the law of the Lord, *'a pair of turtledoves, or two young pigeons'* (*Lk* 2:21-24). "Jesus' circumcision, on the eighth day after His birth, is the sign of His incorporation into Abraham's descendants, into the people of the covenant. It is the sign of His submission to the Law" (*CCC*, 527).

Our Father, 10 Hail Mary's (contemplating the mystery),
Glory be to the Father.

5. The Finding of the Boy Jesus in the Temple

"Now His parents went to Jerusalem every year at the feast of the Passover. And when He was twelve years old, they went up according to custom; and when the feast was ended, as they were returning, the boy Jesus stayed behind in Jerusalem. His parents did not know it ... After three days they found Him in the temple, sitting among the teachers, listening to them and asking them questions; and all who heard Him were amazed at His understanding and His answers" (*Lk* 2:41-47). "The *finding of Jesus in the temple* is the only event that breaks the silence of the Gospels about the hidden years of Jesus. Here Jesus lets us catch a glimpse of the mystery of His total consecration to a mission that flows from His divine sonship: 'Did you not know that I must be about my Father`s work?' (*Lk* 2:49)" (CCC, 534).

Our Father, 10 Hail Mary's (contemplating the mystery),
Glory be to the Father. *(turn to p.42)*

∞∞∞∞∞ **The Mysteries of Light** ∞∞∞∞∞

1. The Baptism in the Jordan River

"And when Jesus was baptized, He went up immediately from the water, and behold, the heavens were opened and he saw the Spirit of God descending like a dove, and alighting on him; and lo, a voice from heaven, saying, 'This is my beloved Son, with whom I am well-pleased'" (*Mt* 3:16-17). "Jesus' public life begins with His baptism by John in the Jordan. John preaches 'a baptism of repentance for the forgiveness of sins' (*Lk* 3:3)" (*CCC,* 535).

Our Father, 10 Hail Mary's (contemplating the mystery),
Glory be to the Father.

2. The Wedding Banquet in Cana

"On the third day there was a marriage at Cana in Galilee, and the mother of Jesus was there; Jesus also was invited to the marriage, with His disciples. When the wine failed, the mother of Jesus said to him, 'They have no wine.' And Jesus said to her, 'O woman, what have you to do with me? My hour has not yet come.' His mother said to the servants, 'Do whatever He tells you'" (Jn 2:1-5). "On the threshold of His public life Jesus performs His first sign at His mother's request - during a wedding feast: The Church attaches great importance to Jesus' presence at the wedding at Cana. She sees in it the confirmation of the goodness of marriage and the proclamation that thenceforth marriage will be an efficacious sign of Christ's presence" (CCC, 1613).

Our Father, 10 Hail Mary's (contemplating the mystery),
Glory be to the Father.

3. The Proclamation of the Kingdom

"The time is fulfilled, and the kingdom of God is at hand; repent, and believe in the gospel" (Mk 1:15). *"Everyone* is called to enter the Kingdom. First announced to the children of Israel, this messianic kingdom is intended to accept men of all nations" (*CCC,* 543).

Our Father, 10 Hail Mary's (contemplating the mystery),
Glory be to the Father.

4. The Transfiguration

"And after six days Jesus took with Him Peter and James and John his brother, and led them up a high mountain apart. And He was transfigured before them, and His face shone like the sun, and His garments became white as light" (*Mt* 17:1-2). "For a moment Jesus discloses His divine glory, confirming Peter's confession. He also reveals that He will have to go by the way of the cross at Jerusalem in order to 'enter into His glory' (*Lk* 24:26)" (CCC, 555).

Our Father, 10 Hail Mary's contemplating the mystery),
Glory be to the Father.

5.   *The Institution of the Holy Eucharist*

"Now as they were eating, Jesus took bread, and blessed, and broke it, and gave it to the disciples and said, 'Take, eat; this is my body'" (*Mt* 26:26). "By celebrating the Last Supper with His Apostles in the course of the Passover meal, Jesus gave the Jewish Passover its definitive meaning. Jesus' passing over to His Father by His Death and Resurrection, the new Passover, is anticipated in the Supper and celebrated in the Eucharist, which fulfills the Jewish Passover and anticipates the final Passover of the Church in the glory of the Kingdom" (CCC, 1340).

Our Father, 10 Hail Mary's (contemplating the mystery),
Glory be to the Father. *(turn to p.42)*

∞∞∞∞∞ **The Sorrowful Mysteries** ∞∞∞∞∞

1.   *The Agony in the Garden*

"Then Jesus went with them to a place called Gethsemane, and He said to His disciples, 'Sit here, while I go yonder and pray.' And taking with Him Peter and the two sons of Zebedee, He began to be sorrowful and troubled. Then He said to them, 'My soul is very sorrowful, even to death; remain here, and watch with me.' And going a little farther He fell on His face and prayed, 'My Father, if it be possible, let this cup pass from me; nevertheless, not as I will, but as You will'" (*Mt* 26:36-39). "Such a battle and such a victory become possible only through prayer. It is by His prayer that Jesus vanquishes the Tempter, both at the outset of His public mission and in the ultimate struggle of His agony" (*CCC*, 2849).

Our Father, 10 Hail Mary's (contemplating the mystery),
Glory be to the Father.

2.   *The scourging at the Pillar*

"Then Pilate took Jesus and scourged him. And the soldiers plaited a crown of thorns, and put it on His head, and arrayed Him in a purple robe; they came up to him, saying, 'Hail, King of the Jews!' and struck Him with their hands" (Jn 19:1-3). "Jesus' sufferings took their historical, concrete form from the fact that He was 'rejected by the elders and the chief priests and the scribes' (Mk 8:31), who 'handed

Him to the Gentiles to be mocked and scourged and crucified'
(*Mt* 20:19)" (CCC, 572).

Our Father, 10 Hail Mary's (contemplating the mystery),
Glory be to the Father.

3.   *The Crowning of Thorns*

"Then the soldiers of the governor took Jesus into the praetorium, and
they gathered the whole battalion before him. And they stripped Him
and put a scarlet robe upon him, and plaiting a crown of thorns they put
it on His head, and put a reed in His right hand. And kneeling before
Him they mocked him, saying, 'Hail, King of the Jews!'" (Mt 27:27-
29). "It is love 'to the end' (Jn 13:1) that confers on Christ's sacrifice its
value as redemption and reparation, as atonement and satisfaction. He
knew and loved us all when He offered His life" (*CCC*, 616).

Our Father, 10 Hail Mary's (contemplating the mystery),
Glory be to the Father.

4.   *The Carrying of the Cross*

"And they compelled a passer-by, Simon of Cyrene, who was coming
in from the country, the father of Alexander and Rufus, to carry His
cross. And they brought Him to the place called Golgotha (which
means the place of a skull)" (Mk 15:21-22). "By accepting in His
human will that the Father's will be done, He accepts His death as
redemptive, for 'he himself bore our sins in His body on the tree'
(1 *Pt* 2:24)" (*CCC*, 612).

Our Father, 10 Hail Mary's (contemplating the mystery),
Glory be to the Father.

5.   *The Crucifixion and Death of Our Lord*

"And when they came to the place which is called The Skull, there they
crucified him, and the criminals, one on the right and one on the left.
And Jesus said, 'Father, forgive them; for they know not what they do'.
It was now about the sixth hour, and there was darkness over the whole
land until the ninth hour, while the sun's light failed; and the curtain of
the temple was torn in two. Then Jesus, crying with a loud voice, said,
'Father, into thy hands I commit my spirit!' And having said this He

breathed His last" (*Lk* 23:33-46). "'Christ died for our sins in accordance with the scriptures' (1 *Cor* 15:3)" (CCC, 619).

Our Father, 10 Hail Mary's (contemplating the mystery),
Glory be to the Father. *(turn to p.42)*

∞∞∞∞∞ **The Glorious Mysteries** ∞∞∞∞∞

1.   *The Resurrection of Jesus from the Dead*

"But on the first day of the week, at early dawn, they went to the tomb, taking the spices which they had prepared. And they found the stone rolled away from the tomb, but when they went in they did not find the body. While they were perplexed about this, behold, two men stood by them in dazzling apparel; and as they were frightened and bowed their faces to the ground, the men said to them, 'Why do you seek the living among the dead? He is not here, but has risen'" (Lk 24:1-5). "'If Christ has not been raised, then our preaching is in vain and your faith is in vain' (1 *Cor* 15:14). The Resurrection above all constitutes the confirmation of all Christ's works and teachings" (*CCC*, 651).

Our Father, 10 Hail Mary's (contemplating the mystery),
Glory be to the Father.

2.   *The Ascension of Our Lord into Heaven*

"So then the Lord Jesus, after He had spoken to them, was taken up into heaven, and sat down at the right hand of God" (Mk 16:19). "This final stage stays closely linked to the first, that is, to His descent from heaven in the Incarnation. Only the one who 'came from the Father' can return to the Father: Christ Jesus" (*CCC*, 661).

Our Father, 10 Hail Mary's (contemplating the mystery),
Glory be to the Father.

3.   *The Descent of the Holy Spirit*

"When the day of Pentecost had come, they were all together in one place. And suddenly a sound came from heaven like the rush of a mighty wind, and it filled the entire house where they were sitting. And there appeared to them tongues as of fire, distributed and resting on each one of them. And they were all filled with the Holy Spirit and began to speak in other tongues, as the Spirit gave them utterance" (Acts 2:1-4). "'Holy Spirit' is the proper name of the one whom we adore and glorify with the Father and the Son. The Church has received this name from the Lord and professes it in the Baptism of her new children" (CCC, 691).

Our Father, 10 Hail Mary's (contemplating the mystery),
Glory be to the Father.

4.   The Assumption of the Virgin Mary, Body and Soul, into Heaven.

"Henceforth all generations will call me blessed; for He who is mighty has done great things for me" (*Lk* 1:48-49). "The Most Blessed Virgin Mary, when the course of her earthly life was completed, was taken up body and soul into the glory of heaven, where she already shares in the glory of her Son's Resurrection, anticipating the resurrection of all members of His Body" (*CCC*, 974).

Our Father, 10 Hail Mary's (contemplating the mystery),
Glory be to the Father.

5.   The Crowing of Mary as Queen of Heaven

"And a great portent appeared in heaven, a woman clothed with the sun, with the moon under her feet, and on her head a crown of twelve stars" (*Rev* 12:1). "Finally the Immaculate Virgin, preserved free from all stain of original sin, when the course of her earthly life was finished, was taken up body and soul into heavenly glory, and exalted by the Lord as Queen over all things, so that she might be the more fully conformed to her Son, the Lord of lords and conqueror of sin and death" (*CCC,* 966).

Our Father, 10 Hail Mary's (contemplating the mystery),
Glory be to the Father. (Continue to p.42)

THE CONCLUSION OF THE ROSARY

R: *Hail, holy Queen,*
ALL: Mother of mercy; hail, our life, our sweetness and our hope. To thee do we cry, poor banished children of Eve; to thee do we send up our sighs, mourning and weeping in this valley of tears. Turn then, most gracious advocate, thine eyes of mercy towards us; and after this our exile, show unto us the blessed fruit of thy womb, Jesus. O clement, O loving, O sweet Virgin Mary.

L: *Pray for us O Holy Mother of God*
R: That we might be made worthy of
        the promises of God.

L: *Let us Pray.*

ALL: O God whose only begotten Son by His life, death, and Resurrection has purchased for us the rewards of eternal life; grant we beseech thee, that meditating on these mysteries of the Most Holy Rosary of the Blessed Virgin Mary, we may imitate what they contain and obtain what they promise through the same Christ our Lord. Amen.

ᵒᵒᵒ
Litany of the Blessed Virgin Mary

Lord have mercy on us.	*Lord have mercy on us.*
Christ have mercy on us.	*Christ have mercy on us.*
Lord have mercy on us.	*Lord have mercy on us.*
Christ, hear us.	*Christ, graciously hear us.*
God the Father of Heaven,	*have mercy on us.*
God the Son, Redeemer of the world,	*have mercy on us.*
God the Holy Ghost,	*have mercy on us.*
Holy Trinity, one God,	*have mercy on us.*
Holy Mary,	*pray for us*
Holy Mother of God,	*pray for us*
Holy Virgin of virgins,	*pray for us*
Mother of Christ,	*pray for us*
Mother of divine grace,	*pray for us*
Mother most pure,	*pray for us*
Mother most chaste,	*pray for us*

Mother inviolate,	*pray for us*
Mother undefiled,	*pray for us*
Mother most amiable,	*pray for us*
Mother most admirable,	*pray for us*
Mother of good counsel,	*pray for us*
Mother of our Creator,	*pray for us*
Mother of our Redeemer,	*pray for us*
Virgin most prudent,	*pray for us*
Virgin most venerable,	*pray for us*
Virgin most renowned,	*pray for us*
Virgin most powerful,	*pray for us*
Virgin most merciful,	*pray for us*
Virgin most faithful,	*pray for us*
Mirror of justice,	*pray for us*
Seat of wisdom,	*pray for us*
Cause of our joy,	*pray for us*
Spiritual vessel,	*pray for us*
Vessel of honor,	*pray for us*
Singular vessel of devotion,	*pray for us*
Mystical rose,	*pray for us*
Tower of David,	*pray for us*
Tower of ivory,	*pray for us*
House of gold,	*pray for us*
Ark of the covenant,	*pray for us*
Gate of Heaven,	*pray for us*
Morning Star,	*pray for us*
Health of the sick,	*pray for us*
Refuge of sinners,	*pray for us*
Comforter of the afflicted,	*pray for us*
Help of Christians,	*pray for us*
Queen of Angels,	*pray for us*
Queen of Patriarchs,	*pray for us*
Queen of Prophets,	*pray for us*
Queen of Apostles,	*pray for us*
Queen of Martyrs,	*pray for us*
Queen of Confessors,	*pray for us*
Queen of Virgins,	*pray for us*
Queen of all Saints,	*pray for us*
Queen conceived without original sin,	*pray for us*
Queen of the most holy Rosary,	*pray for us*
Queen of peace,	*pray for us*

Lamb of God, Who takes away the sins of the world:
Spare us, O Lord.
Lamb of God, Who takes away the sins of the world:
Graciously hear us, O Lord.
Lamb of God, Who takes away the sins of the world:
Have mercy on us.

Pray for us, most holy Mother of God,
That we may be made worthy of the promises of Christ.

During the Year

Let us pray. Grant, we beg you, O Lord God, that we Your servants, may enjoy lasting health of mind and body, and by the glorious intercession of the Blessed Mary, ever Virgin, be delivered from present sorrow and enter into the joy of eternal happiness.
Through Christ our Lord. *R.* Amen.

During Advent

Let us pray. O God, You willed that, at the message of an angel, Your Word should take flesh in the womb of the Blessed Virgin Mary; grant to Your suppliant people, that we, who believe her to be truly the Mother of God, may be helped by her intercession with you.
Through the same Christ our Lord. *R.* Amen.

From Christmas to the Purification

Let us pray. O God, by the fruitful virginity of Blessed Mary, you bestowed upon the human race the rewards of eternal salvation; grant, we beg you, that we may feel the power of her intercession, through whom we have been made worthy to receive the Author of life, our Lord Jesus Christ Your Son. Who lives and reigns with You
forever and ever. *R. Amen.*

During Easter Season

Let us pray. O God, who by the Resurrection of Your Son, our Lord Jesus Christ, granted joy to the whole world; grant, we beg you, that through the intercession of the Virgin Mary, His Mother, we may attain the joys of eternal life. Through the same Christ our Lord. *R.* Amen.

Hymns in honor of the Blessed Virgin Mary

The Easter Regina Cæli

Regina cæli, lætare, alleluia:	Queen of Heaven, rejoice, alleluia.
Quia quem meruisti portare, alleluia,	For He whom thou didst merit to bear in your womb, alleluia.
Resurrexit, sicut dixit, alleluia,	Has risen, as He promised, alleluia.
Ora pro nobis Deum, alleluia.	Pray for us to God, alleluia.

Salve, Regina

Salve, Regina, Mater Misericordiae; vita, ducedo et spes nostra, salve.	Hail, holy Queen, Mother of Mercy, our life, our sweetness and our hope.
Ad te clamamus exsules filii Hevae. Ad te suspiramus gementes et flentes in hac lacrimarum valle.	To thee do we cry, poor banished children of Eve; to thee do we send up our sighs, mourning and weeping in this valley of tears.
Eia ergo, advocata nostra, illos tuos misericordes oculos ad nos converte. Et Iesum, benedictum fructum ventris tui, nobis post hoc exsilium ostende.	Turn then, most gracious advocate, thine eyes of mercy toward us; and after this our exile, show unto us the blessed fruit of thy womb, Jesus.
O clemens, o pia, o dulcis Virgo Maria.	O clement, O loving, O sweet Virgin Mary.

THE STATIONS OF THE CROSS

✝

St. Alphonsus Liguori

Preparatory Prayer

ALL: My Lord, Jesus Christ, / You have made this journey to die for me with unspeakable love; / and I have so many times ungratefully abandoned You. / But now I love You with all my heart; / and, because I love You, I am sincerely sorry for ever having offended You. / Pardon me, my God, and permit me to accompany You on this journey. / You go to die for love of me; / I want, my beloved Redeemer, to die for love of You. / My Jesus, I will live and die always united to You.

At the cross her station keeping / Stood the mournful Mother weeping
Close to Jesus to the last

1.   Pilate Condemns Jesus to Die

L: We adore You, O Christ, and we praise You. (*Genuflect*)
R: Because, by Your holy cross,
You have redeemed the world. (*Rise*)

L: Consider how Jesus Christ, after being scourged and crowned with thorns, was unjustly condemned by Pilate to die on the cross. (*Kneel*)

R: My adorable Jesus, / it was not Pilate; / no, it was my sins that condemned You to die. / I beseech You, by the merits of this sorrowful journey, / to assist my soul on its journey to eternity./ I love You, beloved Jesus; / I love You more than I love myself. / With all my heart I repent of ever having offended You. / Grant that I may love You always; and then do with me as You will.

(Our Father, Hail Mary, Glory be.)
Through her heart, His sorrow sharing / All His bitter anguish bearing
Now at length the sword has passed

2. Jesus Accepts His Cross

L: We adore You, O Christ, and we praise You. (*Genuflect*)
R: Because, by Your holy cross, You have redeemed the world. (*Rise*)

L: Consider Jesus as He walked this road with the cross on His shoulders, thinking of us, and offering to His Father in our behalf, the death He was about to suffer. (*Kneel*)

R: My most beloved Jesus, / I embrace all the sufferings You have destined for me until death. / I beg You, by all You suffered in carrying Your cross, / to help me carry mine with Your perfect peace and resignation. / I love You, Jesus, my love; / I repent of ever having offended You. / Never let me separate myself from You again. / Grant that I may love You always; and then do with me as You will.

(*Our Father, Hail Mary, Glory be.*)

O, how sad and sore depressed / Was that Mother highly blessed
Of the sole Begotten One

3. Jesus Falls the First Time

L: We adore You, O Christ, and we praise You. (*Genuflect*)
R: Because, by Your holy cross, You have redeemed the world. (*Rise*)

L: Consider the first fall of Jesus. Loss of blood from the scourging and crowing with thorns had so weakened Him that He could hardly walk; and yet He had to carry that great load upon His shoulders. As the soldiers struck Him cruelly, He fell several times under the heavy cross. (*Kneel*)

R: My beloved Jesus, / it was not the weight of the cross / but the weight of my sins which made You suffer so much. / By the merits of this first fall, / save me from falling into mortal sin. / I love You, O my Jesus, with all my heart; / I am sorry that I have offended You. / May I never offend You again. / Grant that I may love You always; and then do with me as You will.

(*Our Father, Hail Mary, Glory be.*)

Christ above in torment hangs / She beneath beholds the pangs
Of her dying, glorious Son

4.   Jesus Meets His Afflicted Mother

L: We adore You, O Christ, and we praise You. (*Genuflect*)
R: Because, by Your holy cross, You have redeemed the world. (*Rise*)

L: Consider how the Son met His Mother on His way to Calvary. Jesus and Mary gazed at each other and their looks became as so many arrows to wound those hearts which loved each other so tenderly (*Kneel*)

R: My most loving Jesus, / by the pain You suffered in this meeting / grant me the grace of being truly devoted to Your most holy Mother. / And You, my Queen, who was overwhelmed with sorrow, / obtain for me by Your prayers / a tender and a lasting remembrance of the passion of Your divine Son. / I love You, Jesus, my Love, above all things. / I repent of ever having offended You. / Never allow me to offend You again. / Grant that I may love You always; and then do with me as You will.

(*Our Father, Hail Mary, Glory be.*)

Is there one who would not weep, / 'whelmed in miseries so deep
Christ's dear Mother to behold.

5.   Simon Helps Jesus Carry the Cross

L: We adore You, O Christ, and we praise You. (*Genuflect*)
R: Because, by Your holy cross, You have redeemed the world. (*Rise*)

L: Consider how weak and weary Jesus was. At each step He was at the point of expiring. Fearing that He would die on the way when they wished Him to die the infamous death of the cross, they forced Simon of Cyrene to help carry the cross after Our Lord. (*Kneel*)

R: My beloved Jesus / I will not refuse the cross as Simon did: / I accept it and embrace it. / I accept in particular the death that is destined for me / with all the pains that may accompany it. / I unite it to Your death / and I offer it to You. / You have died for love of me; / I will die for love of You and to please You. / Help me by Your grace. / I love You, Jesus, my Love; / I repent of ever having offended You. /

Never let me offend You again. / Grant that I may love You always; and then do with me as You will.

(Our Father, Hail Mary, Glory be.)

Can the human heart refrain / From partaking in her pain
In that Mother's pain untold?

6.   Veronica Offers Her Veil to Jesus

L: We adore You, O Christ, and we praise You. (*Genuflect*)
R: Because, by Your holy cross, You have redeemed the world. (*Rise*)

L: Consider the compassion of the holy woman, Veronica. Seeing Jesus in such distress, His face bathed in sweat and blood, she presented Him with her veil. Jesus wiped His face, and left upon the cloth the image of His sacred countenance. (*Kneel*)

R: My beloved Jesus, / Your face was beautiful before You began this journey; / but, now, it no longer appears beautiful / and is disfigured with wounds and blood. / Alas, my soul also was once beautiful / when it received Your grace in Baptism; / but I have since disfigured it with my sins. / You alone, my Redeemer, can restore it to its former beauty. / Do this by the merits of Your passion; and then do with me as You will.

(Our Father, Hail Mary, Glory be.)

Bruised, derided, cursed, defiled / She beheld her tender Child
All with bloody scourges rent.

7.   Jesus Falls the Second Time

L: We adore You, O Christ, and we praise You. (*Genuflect*)
R: Because, by Your holy cross, You have redeemed the world. (*Rise*)

L: Consider how the second fall of Jesus under His cross renews the pain in all the wounds of the head and members of our afflicted Lord. (*Kneel*)

R: My most gentle Jesus, / how many times You have forgiven me; / and how many times I have fallen again and begun again to offend

You! / By the merits of this second fall, / give me the grace to persevere in Your love until death. / Grant, that in all my temptations, I may always have recourse to You. / I love You, Jesus, my Love with all my heart; / I am sorry that I have offended You. / Never let me offend You again. / Grant that I may love You always; and then do with me as You will.

(Our Father, Hail Mary, Glory be.)

For the sins of His own nation / Saw Him hang in desolation
Till His spirit forth He sent.

8. Jesus Speaks to the Women

L: We adore You, O Christ, and we praise You. (*Genuflect*)
R: Because, by Your holy cross, You have redeemed the world. (*Rise*)

L: Consider how the women wept with compassion seeing Jesus so distressed and dripping with blood as He walked along. Jesus said to them, ``Weep not so much for me, but rather for Your children." (*Kneel*)

R: My Jesus, laden with sorrows, / I weep for the sins which I have committed against You / because of the punishment I deserve for them; / and, still more, because of the displeasure they have caused You / who have loved me with an infinite love. / It is Your love, more than the fear of hell, / which makes me weep for my sins. / My Jesus, I love You more than myself; / I am sorry that I have offended You. / Never allow me to offend You again. / Grant that I may love You always; and then do with me as You will.

(Our Father, Hail Mary, Glory be.)

O sweet Mother! Fount of Love, / Touch my spirit from above
Make my heart with yours accord.

9. Jesus Falls the Third Time

L: We adore You, O Christ, and we praise You. (*Genuflect*)
R: Because, by Your holy cross, You have redeemed the world. (*Rise*)

L: Consider how Jesus Christ fell for the third time. He was extremely weak and the cruelty of His executioners was excessive; they tried to hasten His steps though He hardly had strength to move. (*Kneel*)

R: My outraged Jesus, / by the weakness You suffered in going to Calvary, / give me enough strength to overcome all human respect / and all my evil passions which have led me to despise Your friendship. / I love You, Jesus my Love, with all my heart; / I am sorry for ever having offended You. / Never permit me to offend You again. / Grant that I may love You always; and then do with me as You will.

(*Our Father, Hail Mary, Glory be.*)

Make me feel as You have felt / Make my soul to glow and melt
With the love of Christ, my Lord.

10. Jesus Is Stripped of His Garments

L: We adore You, O Christ, and we praise You. (*Genuflect*)
R: Because, by Your holy cross, You have redeemed the world. (*Rise*)

L: Consider how Jesus was violently stripped of His clothes by His executioners. The inner garments adhered to His lacerated flesh and the soldiers tore them off so roughly that the skin came with them. Have pity for your Savior so cruelly treated and tell Him: (*Kneel*)

R: My innocent Jesus, / by the torment You suffered in being stripped of Your garments, / help me to strip myself of all attachment for the things of earth / that I may place all my love in You who are so worthy of my love. / I love You, O Jesus, with all my heart; / I am sorry for ever having offended You. / Never let me offend You again. / Grant that I may love You always; and then do with me as You will.

(*Our Father, Hail Mary, Glory be.*)

Holy Mother, pierce me through / In my heart each wound renew
Of my Savior crucified

11.   Jesus Is Nailed to the Cross

L: We adore You, O Christ, and we praise You. (*Genuflect*)
R: Because, by Your holy cross, You have redeemed the world. (*Rise*)

L: Consider Jesus, thrown down upon the cross, He stretched out His arms and offered to His eternal Father the sacrifice of His life for our salvation. They nailed His hands and feet, and then, raising the cross, left Him to die in anguish. (*Kneel*)

R: My despised Jesus, / nail my heart to the cross / that it may always remain there to love You and never leave You again. / I love You more than myself; / I am sorry for ever having offended You. / Never permit me to offend You again. / Grant that I may love You always; and then do with me as You will.

(*Our Father, Hail Mary, Glory be.*)

*Let me share with you His pain, / Who for all our sins was slain,
Who for me in torments died.*

12.   Jesus Dies Upon the Cross

L: We adore You, O Christ, and we praise You. (*Genuflect*)
R: Because, by Your holy cross, You have redeemed the world. (*Rise*)

L: Consider how Your Jesus, after three hours of agony on the cross, is finally overwhelmed with suffering and, abandoning Himself to the weight of His body, bows His head and dies. (*Kneel*)

R: My dying Jesus, / I devoutly kiss the cross on which You would die for love of me. / I deserve, because of my sins, to die a terrible death; / but Your death is my hope. / By the merits of Your death, / give me the grace to die embracing Your feet and burning with love of You. / I yield my soul into Your hands. / I love You with my whole heart. / I am sorry that I have offended You. / Never let me offend You again. / Grant that I may love You always; and then do with me as You will.

(*Our Father, Hail Mary, Glory be.*)

*Let me mingle tears with thee / Mourning Him who mourned for me,
All the days that I may live.*

13. Jesus Is Taken Down from the Cross

L: We adore You, O Christ, and we praise You. (*Genuflect*)
R: Because, by Your holy cross, You have redeemed the world. (*Rise*)

L: Consider how, after Our Lord had died, He was taken down from the cross by two of His disciples, Joseph and Nicodemus, and placed in the arms of His afflicted Mother. She received Him with unutterable tenderness and pressed Him close to her bosom. (*Kneel*)

R: O Mother of Sorrows, / for the love of Your Son, / accept me as Your servant and pray to Him for me, / And You, my Redeemer, since You have died for me, / allow me to love You, / for I desire only You and nothing more. / I love You, Jesus my Love, / and I am sorry that I have offended You. / Never let me offend You again. / Grant that I may love You always; and then do with me as You will.

(Our Father, Hail Mary, Glory be.)

By the cross with you to stay / There with you to weep and pray
Is all I ask of you to give.

14. Jesus Is Placed in the Sepulcher

L: We adore You, O Christ, and we praise You. (*Genuflect*)
R: Because, by Your holy cross, You have redeemed the world. (*Rise*)

L: Consider how the disciples carried the body of Jesus to its burial, while His holy Mother went with them and arranged it in the sepulcher with her own hands. They then closed the tomb and all departed. (*Kneel*)

R: Oh, my buried Jesus, / I kiss the stone that closes You in. / But You gloriously did rise again on the third day. / I beg You by Your resurrection that I may be raised gloriously on the last day, / to be united with You in heaven, to praise You and love You forever. / I love You, Jesus, and I repent of ever having offended You. / Grant that I may love You always; and then do with me as You will.

(Our Father, Hail Mary, Glory be.)

Virgin of all virgins blest! / Listen to my fond request:
Let me share your grief divine.

RITE OF EXPOSITION AND ADORATION OF
THE MOST BLESSED SACRAMENT

Exposition of the Blessed Sacrament

Hymn

O saving Victim, open wide
The gate of Heaven
to man below;
Our foes press on
from every side;
Your aid supply;
Your strength bestow.

To Your great name
be endless praise;
Immortal Godhead,
One in Three;
Grant us, for endless
length of days,
In our true native land to be.

O salutaris Hostia
Quae caeli pandis ostium;
Bella premunt hostilia,
Da robur, fer auxilium.

Uni trinoque Domino
Sit sempiterna gloria,
Qui vitam sine termino
Nobis donet in patria. Amen

Period of Adoration

Rite of Benediction

Down in adoration falling,
Lo! the sacred Host we hail,
Lo! oe'r ancient forms departing
Newer rites of grace prevail;
Faith for all defects supplying,
Where the feeble senses fail.

To the everlasting Father,
And the Son Who reigns on high
With the Holy Spirit proceeding
Forth from each eternally,
Be salvation, honor blessing,
Might and endless majesty.
Amen.

Tantum ergo Sacramentum
Veneremur cernui:
Et antiquum documentum
Novo cedat ritui:
Praestet fides supplementum
Sensuum defectui.

Genitori, Genitoque
Laus et jubilatio,
Salus, honor, virtus quoque
Sit et benedictio:
Procedenti ab utroque
Compar sit laudatio.
Amen.

Let us pray.

Orémus.

Lord Jesus Christ,
You gave us the Eucharist
as the memorial
of Your suffering and death.
May our worship of this sacrament
of Your Body and Blood
help us to experience the salvation
You won for us and the peace of
the kingdom where You live with
the Father and the Holy Spirit,
one God, for ever and ever. Amen.

Deus, qui nobis, sub sacraménto
mirábili,
passiónis tuæ memóriam
reliquísti:
tríbue, quæsumus; ita nos
Córporis et Sánguinis tui sacra
mystéria venerári, ut redemptiónis
tuæ fructum in nobis júgiter
sentiámus:
Qui vivis et regnas in sæcula
sæculórum. Amen

Eucharistic Blessing and Divine Praises

Blessed be God.
Blessed be His holy Name.
Blessed be Jesus Christ, true God
and true Man.
Blessed be the Name of Jesus.
Blessed be His most Sacred Heart.
Blessed be his most Precious Blood.
Blessed be Jesus in the most Holy
Sacrament of the Altar.
Blessed be the Holy Spirit, the
Comforter.

Blessed be the great Mother of God,
Mary most holy.
Blessed be her holy
and immaculate conception
Blessed be her glorious assumption.
Blessed be the name of Mary,
Virgin and Mother.
Blessed be Saint Joseph, her most
chaste spouse. Blessed be God in
His angels and in His saints.

Repose of the Blessed Sacrament

Hymn

Holy God, we praise thy Name;
Lord of all, we bow before thee!
All on earth thy scepter claim,
All in Heaven above adore thee;
Infinite thy vast domain,
Everlasting is thy reign.

Hark! the loud celestial hymn
Angel choirs above are raising,
Cherubim and seraphim,
In unceasing chorus praising;
Fill the heavens
Holy, holy, holy Lord

Holy Father, Holy Son, Holy Spirit,
Three we name thee;
While in essence only One,
Undivided God we claim thee;
And adoring bend the knee,
While we own the mystery.

THE SACRED HEART OF JESUS

Dedication

O Jesus, through the Immaculate Heart of Mary,
I offer You my prayers, works, joys and sufferings of this day for all
the intentions of Your Sacred Heart, in union with the Holy Sacrifice of
the Mass throughout the world, in reparation for my sins, and for the
intentions of our Holy Father the Pope. Amen

Prayer of Offering

My loving Savior,
consume my heart in
that burning love with which
Your own Heart is inflamed.
Pour out upon me those graces
which flow from Your love.

Let my heart be
so united with yours
that our wills

may be one, and my will
may in all things
be conformed with Your will.

May Your will be the guide
and rule of my desires
and of my actions.

Amen

Prayer for those in need

Lord Jesus Christ,
Your Heart still cherishes
all the redeemed
and is moved to pity
for every human need.

Aware of Your invitation,
"Come to Me,"
we pray for the afflicted,
the sick, the confused,
for all broken hearts,
and shattered lives.

We bring to You all their
material, emotional, and
spiritual needs
as well as our own.

By the love that led You
to take flesh of
the Virgin Mary,
we pray that You might
enfold us all
in Your merciful love,
heal our wounds
and grant us what accords with
Your holy will.

To the Sacred Heart of Jesus

Most kind Jesus,
Redeemer of the human race,
look down upon us
humbly prostrate before you.
We are yours,
and yours we wish to be;
but to be more
surely united with you,
each one of us freely
consecrate ourselves today
to Your Most Sacred Heart.

Many indeed have
never known you;
many, too,
despising Your precepts,
have rejected you.
Have mercy on them all,
most merciful Jesus,
and draw them to
Your Sacred Heart.

Be King, O Lord,
not only of the faithful
who have never forsaken you,
but also of the prodigal
children who have
abandoned you;
Grant that they may quickly

return to their Father's house,
lest they die
of wretchedness and hunger.

Be King of those who are
deceived by erroneous
opinions,
or whom discord keeps aloof,
and call them back
to the harbor of truth
and the unity of faith,
so that soon there may be
but one flock and one
Shepherd.

Grant, O Lord, to Your Church
assurance of freedom
and immunity from harm;
give tranquility of order
to all nations;
make the earth resound
from pole to pole with one cry:

Praise to the divine Heart
that wrought our salvation;
to It be glory and honor for
ever. Amen.

Litany of the Sacred Heart

Lord, have mercy.
Lord, have mercy.

Christ, have mercy.
Christ, have mercy.

Lord, have mercy.
Lord, have mercy

Christ, hear us.
Christ, graciously hear us.

God, the Father of Heaven,
have mercy on us.
God, the Son,
Redeemer of the world,
have mercy on us.
God, the Holy Spirit,
have mercy on us.
Holy Trinity, one God,
have mercy on us.
Heart of Jesus,
Son of the Eternal Father,
have mercy on us.
Heart of Jesus, formed in the
womb of the Virgin Mother
by the Holy Spirit,
have mercy on us.
Heart of Jesus,
united substantially to the
Word of God,
have mercy on us.
Heart of Jesus,
of infinite majesty,
have mercy on us.
Heart of Jesus,
holy temple of God,
have mercy on us.
Heart of Jesus,
tabernacle of the Most High,
have mercy on us.
Heart of Jesus,
house of God and
gate of heaven,
have mercy on us.
Heart of Jesus,
glowing furnace of charity,
have mercy on us.
Heart of Jesus,
vessel of justice and love,
have mercy on us.

Heart of Jesus,
full of goodness and love,
have mercy on us.
Heart of Jesus,
abyss of all virtues,
have mercy on us.
Heart of Jesus,
most worthy of all praise,
have mercy on us.

Heart of Jesus,
king and center of all hearts,
have mercy on us.
Heart of Jesus, in whom are
all the treasures of
wisdom and knowledge,
have mercy on us.
Heart of Jesus, in whom dwells
all the fullness of the Divinity,
have mercy on us.
Heart of Jesus, in whom the
Father is well pleased,
have mercy on us.
Heart of Jesus,
of whose fullness
we have all received,
have mercy on us.
Heart of Jesus, desire of
the everlasting hills,
have mercy on us.

Heart of Jesus, patient and
rich in mercy,
have mercy on us.
Heart of Jesus,
rich to all who invoke you,
have mercy on us.
Heart of Jesus,
fount of life and holiness,
have mercy on us.

Heart of Jesus,
propitiation for our sins,
have mercy on us.
Heart of Jesus,
saturated with reviling,
have mercy on us.
Heart of Jesus,
crushed for our iniquities,
have mercy on us.
Heart of Jesus,
made obedient unto death,
have mercy on us.
Heart of Jesus,
pierced with a lance,
have mercy on us.
Heart of Jesus,
source of all consolation,
have mercy on us.
Heart of Jesus,
our life and resurrection,
have mercy on us.
Heart of Jesus,
our peace and reconciliation,
have mercy on us.

Heart of Jesus,
victim for our sins,
have mercy on us.
Heart of Jesus, salvation of
those who hope in you,
have mercy on us.
Heart of Jesus,
hope of those who die in you,
have mercy on us.
Heart of Jesus,
delight of all saints,
have mercy on us.

Lamb of God, You take away
the sins of the world,
spare us, O Lord.
Lamb of God, You take away
the sins of the world,
graciously hear us, O Lord.
Lamb of God, You take away
the sins of the world,
have mercy on us
Jesus, meek and
humble of Heart.
*Make our hearts like
onto Thine*

Let us pray

Almighty and everlasting God, look upon the Heart of Your well
beloved Son and upon the acts of praise and satisfaction which He
renders to You in the name of sinners.

Of Your great goodness, grant pardon to those who seek Your
mercy, in the name of the Your Son, Jesus Christ, who lives and reigns
with you, forever and ever. Amen

LITANIES

Litany of the Holy Name of Jesus

Lord, have mercy.
Lord, have mercy.
Christ, have mercy.
Christ, have mercy.
Lord, have mercy.
Lord, have mercy
Christ, hear us.
Christ, graciously hear us.

God, the Father of Heaven,
have mercy on us.
God, the Son,
Redeemer of the world,
have mercy on us.
God, the Holy Spirit,
have mercy on us.
Holy Trinity, one God,
have mercy on us.

Jesus, Son of the living God,
have mercy on us.
Jesus, splendor of the Father,
have mercy on us.
Jesus, brightness
of eternal light,
have mercy on us.
Jesus, King of glory,
have mercy on us.
Jesus, sun of justice,
have mercy on us.
Jesus, Son of the Virgin Mary,
have mercy on us.
Jesus, most amiable,
have mercy on us.
Jesus, most admirable,
have mercy on us.

Jesus, the mighty God,
have mercy on us.
Jesus, Father of
the world to come,
have mercy on us.
Jesus, angel of great counsel,
have mercy on us.

Jesus, most powerful,
have mercy on us.
Jesus, most patient,
have mercy on us.
Jesus, most obedient,
have mercy on us.
Jesus, meek and
humble of heart,
have mercy on us.
Jesus, lover of chastity,
have mercy on us.
Jesus, lover of us,
have mercy on us.
Jesus, God of peace,
have mercy on us.

Jesus, author of life,
have mercy on us.
Jesus, example of virtues,
have mercy on us.
Jesus, zealous lover of souls,
have mercy on us.
Jesus, our God,
have mercy on us.
Jesus, our refuge,
have mercy on us.
Jesus, father of the poor,
have mercy on us.

Jesus, treasure of the faithful,
have mercy on us.
Jesus, good Shepherd,
have mercy on us.
Jesus, true light,
have mercy on us.
Jesus, eternal wisdom,
have mercy on us.
Jesus, infinite goodness,
have mercy on us.
Jesus, our way and our life,
have mercy on us.
Jesus, joy of Angels,
have mercy on us.
Jesus, King of the Patriarchs,
have mercy on us.
Jesus, Master of the Apostles,
have mercy on us.
Jesus, teacher of the
Evangelists,
have mercy on us.
Jesus, strength of Martyrs,
have mercy on us.
Jesus, light of Confessors,
have mercy on us.
Jesus, purity of Virgins,
have mercy on us.
Jesus, crown of Saints,
have mercy on us.

Be merciful,
spare us, O Jesus.

Be merciful,
graciously hear us, O Jesus.

From all evil,
deliver us, O Jesus.
From all sin,
deliver us, O Jesus.

From Your wrath,
deliver us, O Jesus
From the snares of the devil,
deliver us, O Jesus.
From the spirit of fornication,
deliver us, O Jesus..
From everlasting death,
deliver us, O Jesus.
From the neglect
of Your inspirations,
deliver us, O Jesus.
By the mystery of
Your holy Incarnation,
deliver us, O Jesus.
By Your Nativity,
deliver us, O Jesus.
By Your Infancy,
deliver us, O Jesus.
By Your most divine Life,
deliver us, O Jesus.
By Your labors,
deliver us, O Jesus.
By Your agony and passion,
deliver us, O Jesus.
By Your cross and dereliction,
deliver us, O Jesus.
By Your sufferings,
deliver us, O Jesus.
By Your death and burial,
deliver us, O Jesus.
By Your Resurrection,
deliver us, O Jesus.
By Your Ascension,
deliver us, O Jesus..
By Your institution
of the most Holy Eucharist,
deliver us, O Jesus.
By Your joys,
deliver us, O Jesus..
By Your glory,
deliver us, O Jesus

Lamb of God, You take away
the sins of the world,
spare us, O Lord.

Lamb of God, You take away
the sins of the world,
graciously hear us, O Lord.

Lamb of God, You take away
the sins of the world,
have mercy on us.

Jesus, hear us.
Jesus, hear us.
Lord Jesus, hear our prayer.
Lord Jesus, hear our prayer.

Let us pray.

O Lord Jesus Christ,
You have said,
"Ask and you shall receive,
seek, and you shall find, knock,

and it shall be opened to you."
Grant, we beg of You,
to us who ask it,
the gift of
Your most divine love,
that we may ever love You
with our whole heart,
in word and deed,
and never cease praising You.

Give us, O Lord,
as much a lasting fear
as a lasting love
of Your Holy Name,
for You, who live
and are King
for ever and ever,
never fail to govern those
whom You have
solidly established
in Your love.

Amen.

Litany of St. Joseph

Lord, have mercy.
Lord, have mercy.

Christ, have mercy.
Christ, have mercy.

Lord, have mercy.
Lord, have mercy

Christ, hear us.
Christ, graciously hear us.

God, the Father of Heaven,
have mercy on us.

God, the Son,
Redeemer of the world,
have mercy on us.

God, the Holy Spirit,
have mercy on us.

Holy Trinity, one God,
have mercy on us.

Holy Mary,
pray for us.
Saint Joseph,
pray for us.
Illustrious son of David,
pray for us.
Light of the patriarchs,
pray for us.
Spouse of the Mother of God,
pray for us.
Chaste guardian of the Virgin,
pray for us.
Foster-father of
the Son of God,
pray for us.
Watchful defender of Christ,
pray for us.
Head of the Holy Family,
pray for us.
Joseph most just,
pray for us.
Joseph most chaste,
pray for us.
Joseph most prudent,
pray for us.
Joseph most valiant,
pray for us.
Joseph most obedient,
pray for us.
Joseph most faithful,
pray for us.
Mirror of patience,
pray for us.
Lover of poverty,
pray for us.

Model of workmen,
pray for us.
Glory of domestic life,
pray for us.
Guardian of virgins,
pray for us.
Pillar of families,
pray for us.
Solace of the afflicted,
pray for us.
Hope of the sick,
pray for us.
Patron of the dying,
pray for us.
Terror of demons,
pray for us.
Protector of Holy Church,
pray for us.

Lamb of God, You take away
the sins of the world,
spare us, O Lord.

Lamb of God, You take away
the sins of the world,
graciously hear us, O Lord.

Lamb of God, You take away
the sins of the world,
have mercy on us.

He made him
the lord of His household,
*And prince over all his
possessions.*

Let us Pray. **O** God, Who in Your ineffable providence did choose Blessed Joseph to be the spouse of Your most Holy Mother, grant that as we venerate him as our protector on earth, we may deserve to have him as our intercessor in Heaven, You Who lives and reigns forever and ever. Amen.

Litany of Humility

O Jesus! meek and humble of heart,	Hear me.
From the desire of being esteemed,	Deliver me, Jesus.
From the desire of being loved,	Deliver me, Jesus.
From the desire of being extolled,	Deliver me, Jesus.
From the desire of being honored,	Deliver me, Jesus.
From the desire of being praised,	Deliver me, Jesus.
From the desire of being preferred to others,	Deliver me, Jesus.
From the desire of being consulted,	Deliver me, Jesus.
From the desire of being approved,	Deliver me, Jesus.
From the fear of being humiliated,	Deliver me, Jesus.
From the fear of being despised,	Deliver me, Jesus.
From the fear of suffering rebukes,	Deliver me, Jesus.
From the fear of being calumniated,	Deliver me, Jesus.
From the fear of being forgotten,	Deliver me, Jesus.
From the fear of being ridiculed,	Deliver me, Jesus.
From the fear of being wronged,	Deliver me, Jesus.
From the fear of being suspected,	Deliver me, Jesus.
From the fear of being ridiculed,	Deliver me, Jesus.
From the fear of being wronged,	Deliver me, Jesus.
From the fear of being suspected,	Deliver me, Jesus.

That others may be loved more than I,
         Jesus, grant me the grace to desire it.
That others may be esteemed more than I,
         Jesus, grant me the grace to desire it.
That, in the opinion of the world, others may increase
         and I decrease,
         Jesus, grant me the grace to desire it.
That others may be chosen and I set aside,
         Jesus, grant me the grace to desire it.
That others may be praised and I unnoticed,
         Jesus, grant me the grace to desire it.
That others may be preferred to me in everything,
         Jesus, grant me the grace to desire it.
That others may become holier than I,
provided that I may become as holy as I should,
         Jesus, grant me the grace to desire it.

The Six Precepts of the Church

1.   To attend Mass on Sundays and holy days of obligation.
2.   To confess your sins at least once a year.
3.   To receive Holy Communion at least during the Easter Season.
4.   To keep holy the holy days of obligation.
5.   To observe the prescribed days of fasting and abstinence.
6.   To provide for the material needs of the Church.

————————

"All Christians in any state or walk of life are
called to the fullness of Christian life and to
the perfection of charity." *Lumen Gentium, 31*

————————

The Works of Mercy

By works of mercy we come to the help of the physical and spiritual needs of the whole family of God, out of respect for each person's human dignity and recognizing that all our neighbors are brothers and sisters, made in the image and likeness of God.

Corporal

Feeding the hungry.
Drink to the thirsty.
Clothing the naked.
Shelter to the homeless.
Visiting the sick.
Visiting those in jail.
Burying the dead.

Spiritual

Good counsel to the doubting.
Instruction to the ignorant.
Admonishing sinners.
Comforting the afflicted.
Forgiveness of offenses.
Bearing wrongs patiently.
Praying for the living and dead.

Guide for Holy Communion

Holy Communion is reserved for members of the Catholic Church. Although expected to attend Mass every Sunday (unless physically prevented), Catholics are not bond to receive Holy Communion every time they attend, although this is the ideal.

When a Catholic does receive, Holy Communion is offered trusting that the member has frequented Confession as necessary (see p.27), is committed to attending weekly Sunday Mass, is able to give a public witness to their Catholic Faith and, if partnered, the relationship is a true Catholic marriage.

Unless dispensed by reason of age or illness, one is also expected to have had fasted from food or drink (with the exception of water), for at least one hour, prior to reception of Holy Communion.

Those not going up to the altar at this Mass may find comfort and strength using the words of the following prayer, thereby making a personal and spiritual communion.

My Jesus, I believe that You are present
in the most Blessed Sacrament.
I love You above all things and
I desire to receive You into my soul.

Since I cannot now
receive You sacramentally,
come at least spiritually into my heart.
I embrace You as if You have already come,
and unite myself wholly to You.
Never permit me to be separated from You.

Amen.